Self-Forgiveness, Self-Love, and Self-Care

Divine Power Within Yourself

Zelda Bendinger

ISBN 979-8-89243-192-7 (paperback)
ISBN 979-8-89243-193-4 (digital)

Christian Faith Publishing
832 Park Avenue
Meadville, PA 16335
www.christianfaithpublishing.com

Printed in the United States of America

Contents

Introduction...v

Self-Forgiveness 2
Self-Love 10
Self-Care 24
Your Divine Life's Purpose.........................34

Conclusion...39
Acknowledgments 41

Introduction

A few years before turning fifty years old, I felt my life was getting ready to make a tremendous change. As I prayed to God to have full and total control over my life, I surrendered *everything* to Him. I was then led to look into His mirror. I was eager to get to know the woman I have become. The good, the bad, the ugly—all my Self-Truths.

Today, I'm proud of who I see each day as I continue to look into God's mirror. I embrace the Divinely made individual He's created fearfully and wonderfully in His image: ***"I praise you because I am fearfully and wonderfully made; your works are wonderful, I know that full well" (Psalm 139:13–14 NIV)***. Acknowledging my sinful ways and imperfections was challenging yet rewarding. As I made the decision to surrender, I also committed to wanting to begin the work of changing my mindset as I reprioritized everyone and everything in my life, putting myself first and closer to God, focusing on my Self-Forgiveness, Self-Love, and Self-Care. Today, as a fifty-one-year-old woman, I have peace and happiness! I'm now living and no longer surviving or existing. I love myself more now than I have ever loved before, not in a coincided way, however—humble. I know who I am and whose I am.

God put it on my heart to write this book to help others find their Divinely given beauty and purpose for your life, your unique characteristics that make you fearfully and wonderfully made. I have chosen my ascended master to be Jesus, the Son of God. Your ascended master may be Quan Yin, a saint, or some other spiritual or religious figure. Together, you and your chosen ascended master can begin to transform your mindset and begin living your best life each day, starting today!

Self-Forgiveness, Self-Love, and Self-Care are vital. Change is required. Turning hurtful or painful personal life experiences into positive life experiences and how you see others in your life will come at a cost. Are you willing to let go of your old ways and do the work for a greater change within yourself? *Change to become different.* Change will be challenging yet rewarding. As you begin to change how you love yourself, you will also change how you love others unapologetically.

> ***Therefore, since we are surrounded by such a great cloud of witnesses, let us throw off everything that hinders and the sin that so easily entangles. And let us run with perseverance the race marked out for us. (Hebrews 12:1 NIV)***

SELF-FORGIVENESS, SELF-LOVE, AND SELF-CARE

Each of us has characteristics about ourselves that we don't particularly care for. Maybe you wish your hair or eyes were a different color? Someone said you aren't pretty? You don't have the look or what it takes for a particular job? Whatever it is, you must remember that beauty comes from within! And once you begin to see your own inner beauty, what others have to say will no longer hold you prisoner. Self-Forgiveness, Self-Love, and Self-Care will allow you to understand and know your Self-Worth. You will no longer try to survive or exist according to others and their self-perceptions they force upon you.

Learning to befriend yourself is not an easy task to do. We are our own worst critics. Accepting the good about yourself will be easy to see and do. Acknowledging and accepting your Self-Truths, not so easy and will require work and the right tools. *Truths: in accordance with fact: sincerity in action, character and utterance.* The first step you must take is to be willing to commit to yourself in order to truly find out who you truthfully are today, journeying through your past and present life to direct how you control your future, a future of a better you!

For some reason, it's easy to see the wrong in others and hold them accountable for their Self-Truths while deflecting and trying to hide from our own truths. Seldom, slow to encouraging them for the good they do show. Why is it that we choose to do this? Point a single finger at someone judging them, meanwhile choosing to ignore the four fingers pointing back at us, our very own truths.

With the help of the ascended master you feel close to—for example, Jesus, Quan Yin, a saint, or some other spiritual/religious figure—this book will be a guide and provide tools to help you begin the process of a new season of your life! Learning how to transform your mindset of Self-Forgiveness, Self-Love, and Self-Care. Break free from the chains of bondage. Be in control of your own happiness.

Water Your Seed

SELF-FORGIVENESS

Acknowledging your own truths is crucial. If you don't see the truths, you will not be able to address the truths. Seeing your truths will bring back hurts and pains from situations we are taught to put into that closet of skeletons. Some of us have swept them under a rug or just pushed them so far back into our subconscious. To forgive yourself, you will have to be willing to address your truths.

I was going through boxes and bins with photo albums and loose pictures as I wanted to do a slide-show for my fiftieth birthday celebration. I couldn't help but notice how each picture I saw of myself as a child drew me near to them—playing outside with not a care in the world, feeling the joy and happiness from my younger self as I smiled big for the camera. I came across this one picture. I must be four or five years old. My eyes look full of life, my hair braided and wearing a red sweater. According to other pictures, I was riding my push-bike—you know, the ones without pedals and require you to push with your feet.

Must be early spring. The grass looks as if winter has just ended. A calm feeling comes over me.

I decide to take this picture, frame it, and place it on the nightstand next to my bedside. After several weeks of waking up and greeting this beautiful child and saying good night to her nightly, I realized that God was helping me to begin my Self-Forgiveness process, the first of four fingers pointing back at me.

Immediately, I felt like my life was rewinding before my eyes. Memory after memory played in my mind. Realizing that every time a painful or hurtful situation played, I started to feel certain emotions, emotions I wasn't sure what I was feeling as I had been taught to put them away into the closet of skeletons, sweep them under a rug, or push them far back into my subconscious, choosing instead to show strength no matter how much pain or hurt I felt. I questioned, "Why am I feeling these emotions? And what am I really feeling?" I'm one of the most sensitive people in the world. In private, I cry "at the drop of a dime," as some would say. I cannot watch a movie, commercial, TV show or listen to music without tearing up, a lumpy feeling always in my throat as I would speak. Yet I mastered showing strength how it was taught to me in order to show respect for my elders: "Do as I say, not as I do." I never learned how to live in the moment.

I found myself speaking out loud and asking Jesus to help me with addressing how to befriend my feelings and emotions that were beginning to surface. Facing my emotions is foreign territory for me. I had been taught to be strong and not to deal with my emotions. However, I was taught to be a giver, which

I later learned was a form of control—controlling situations so I wouldn't show weakness. Receiving was not a part of my strength. When others had tried to give to me, I would find a way to control the situation, always in love, with my taught strength, unknowingly. I needed for nothing. In truth, I needed all that I could get as I allowed "taught strength" to win every time throughout my life.

As I started to acknowledge and accept my Self-Truths, I found myself all over the place. Sad, mad, happy, smiling, laughing—I could go on. The truths that surfaced with negative energy, I didn't like so much. Mistakes I've made toward myself. Things I've said to myself and believed. Mistakes others have made toward me. Things they've said and I chose to believe, as their opinions mattered. Hurtful and painful words, some said jokingly, some said in a nice, nasty way. How does one even begin to see the light at the end of the tunnel?

For me, changing how I would approach each day for myself is in my control. Words are powerful. I would choose to speak positivity over myself no matter what negativity was to come. And because I've been known and told that I love hard, I owed it to myself to show myself the same hard love, taking back my Divinely given power through Self-Forgiveness, which eventually led to forgiving others.

> *For if you forgive other people*
> *when they sin against you, your*
> *heavenly Father will also for-*

> *give you. But if you do not for-*
> *give others sins, your Father will*
> *not forgive your sins. (Matthew*
> *6:14–15)*

DAILY LIFE-CHANGING AGREEMENTS

A book was shared with me in 2006, *The Four Agreements* by Miguel Ruiz. After reading the book, I didn't agree with everything the author shared. However, I was touched by the concept of the four agreements he shared. I created a document on my computer and titled it "Daily Life-Changing Agreements" and taped the agreements, shared by the author, onto my bathroom mirror as a reminder how to approach each day moving forward.

After several months of putting in the work to do better, I taped a copy on my son's bathroom mirror and my daughter's bathroom mirror—even taped a copy on the guest bathroom mirror—not knowing then the impact this simple tool would have on our lives today. Yes, I currently have the four agreements on all bathroom mirrors throughout my home. I've shared this book with others as it has been and still is a tool used within my home and day-to-day life.

Be Impeccable With Your Word!

Speak with integrity. Say only what you mean. Avoid using words to speak against yourself of gossip about others. Use the power of your word in the direction of truth & love. (Impeccable means: without sin)

Don't Take Anything Personally!

Nothing others do is because of you. What others say and do is a projection of their own reality, their own dream/life. When you are immune to the opinions and actions of others, you won't be the victim of needless suffering.

Don't Make Assumptions!

Find the courage to ask questions and to express what you really want. Communicate with others as clearly as you can to avoid misunderstandings, sadness and drama. With this one agreement, you can completely transform your life.

Always Do Your Best!

Your best is going to change from moment to moment; it will be different when you are healthy as opposed to sick. Under any circumstances, simply do your best and you will avoid self-judgment, self-abuse and regret. (Miguel Ruiz, *The Four Agreements*)

Learning to Self-Forgive is a huge step in the right direction. For one, you will enjoy taking back your Divine power that you may or may not have known you were giving away at no cost. That, too, will need to be forgiven. Commit to yourself daily using the tools I've shared for Self-Forgiveness, or create and find tools that will work for you to stay in a place of positivity as you begin to Self-Forgive.

Again, the work you do for yourself will benefit you to help with the forgiveness of others. You must forgive yourself before you can forgive others. Challenge yourself to do the work of Self-Forgiveness. It will be difficult. The reward: to live freely with clearer truths. You and your own Self-Truths will begin to transform your mindset. Then you will be ready to face yet another finger pointing back at you. The second finger, Self-Love.

LOVE
bears
all things,
hopes
all things,
endures
all things,
Love never ends.

SELF-LOVE

The most confident person you know more than likely doesn't truly love their self. Most of us are taught to "fake it till we make it," becoming someone you're not, causing and impacting us to Self-Sabotage how we Self-Love and love others, leaving us to believe that our happiness should come from others as we continue to survive or exist in life we learn to become selfish, prideful, materialistic, etc., no longer living life but trying to survive or exist in life. We all are sinners. Work must be done to change to do better with your Self-Love and love of others. Once you're able to embrace these statements, you will begin to respect how you Self-Love and love for others.

The love I give and show to others always comes from my heart and with positive energy. How I had been Self-Loving looked a little differently. I made sure I ate, bathed, cleaned my home, children not wanting for anything, etc. I took care of the necessities. Not making myself a priority with love, I had been wearing everyone else's shoes while neglecting my very own. How I would Self-Love needed to change quickly. I refuse to not give myself the same love and positive energy, so I asked myself how I would begin to give and show myself the same love with positive energy. I would start each day with committing to show and speak love and positive energy toward myself with humility yet unapologetically.

I realized I would have to learn how to receive Jesus's love for me. ***"'For I know the plans I have for you,' declares the Lord, 'plans to prosper you and not harm you, plans to give you hope and a future'" (Jeremiah 29:11 NIV).*** Courageously, I'm ready to start to do the work. I'm in a different headspace. The fog has lifted, and I revert back to my tools I implemented in the Self-Forgiveness process. As I revisited my tools, I noticed positive, encouraging energy from quotes and text messages sent from others as I was receiving differently. Prayers were starting to be answered. I created affirmations. Reciting them out loud or to myself almost daily, I began to feel more powerful!

Self-Affirmations, the daily life-changing agreements, and encouragement from quotes and text messages helped me become a better me while giving Jesus His glory! I felt stronger as I had opened my arms and heart to receiving all that Jesus has planned for me, extremely careful, however, to stay grounded in my humility.

> ***Humble yourselves, therefore, under God's mighty hand, that he may lift you up in due time. Cast all your anxiety on him***

***because he cares for you. (1
Peter 5:6–7 NIV)***

When you walk past a mirror, whom do you see? Do you love the person looking back at you? Self-Love will probably be the hardest yet most rewarding process you can do for yourself. Love is one of the greatest gifts you can give to yourself and others. ***"A new command I give you: Love one another. As I have loved you, so you must love one another" (John 13:34 NIV).*** Love is the emotions of peace, protection, happiness, joy, comfort, laughter, and smiles for me.

Think about someone you love or your favorite outfit, pair of shoes, color, or food. Notice how you're feeling. Is your energy beginning to feel free and your heart open to receive all the goodness and positive energy from within? Is your heart beating faster? Feeling blood flowing through your veins throughout your body as your body is beginning to heal from within. Positive energy filling your body from the emotion of love. Love from the thoughts of someone or something you love! Why not give that same energy you feel from love of others and things to yourself? Why not you? You deserve it!

THE LORD GIVES STRENGTH
TO HIS PEOPLE;
THE LORD BLESSES
HIS PEOPLE WITH PEACE.

-PSALM 29:11

Peace

We all get to make decisions. With that said, we must learn to agree to disagree in order to Self-Love. What's suitable for you may not be suitable for someone else and vice versa. When you learn to change how your mind processes your own Self-Love, you will learn to be okay with agreeing to disagree while still loving yourself and others.

Since my words have become important and powerful in my day-to-day life, I needed to find a word to help me to stay focused with how I would Self-Love first. My chosen word: *respect. Respect: to consider worthy of high regard.* Respect is how I would show and give myself love first. Maybe you know someone who believes or think they deserve to be shown and given respect yet directly or indirectly showing you disrespect. One of many generational behaviors learned for me: "Do as I say, and not as I do." One of many generational behaviors taught that I have Self-Forgiven and forgiven others for. Self-Forgiveness for learning to do what I was taught by others, which caused me to carry and continue on with generational behaviors and edging God out (EGO) from His plans for me. Others as I suspect it may have worked for them in their time. Grateful to have been given another chance to Self-Love, I no longer choose EGO. Instead, I choose to release what no longer serves me and choose to receive what is for my good!

Well, here's a case of why not me too. Making this decision, I spoke out loud to myself that I would implement the word *respect* with the greatest gift word *love*. I am worthy! Worthy to receive and be shown respect too! I have decided to continue to follow Jesus, my ascended master! Receive what He has for me *(see Jeremiah 29:11 NIV)*. Not giving or showing myself love first is not an option. And with Jesus's help, I would greater understand my worth as I learned to respect my Self-Truths.

You have the ability to control your Self-Truths with the help of your ascended master, which also required me to learn how to agree to disagree with respect while showing Self-Love first. Respecting others for what they choose to do and how they choose to love themselves. Not allowing their perceptions of me to no longer hinder how I would Self-Love. Respectfully learning to agree to disagree while still loving on others.

Since we are individually Divinely made, our circumstances and situations can or cannot look similar to others. I've always been able to feel others' spirits. And no matter what they were going through, I love so hard. I put on their shoes, again setting my own aside. Jesus said, ***"Carry each other's burdens, and in this way you will fulfill the law of Christ"*** ***(Galatians 6:2 NIV)***. Growing in my spiritual gifts today, I receive God's words differently. I unknowingly begin to edge God out (EGO). Stamp the letter *S* (Super Woman/Strength) onto my chest, and instead of flying high in the sky, I'm on the ground battling. Fighting other's fires without a water hose and water as they stand by and watch, some even adding more fuel to the fire. Because I heard from

Jesus and I love hard, I unknowingly take control of the situation by putting on others' shoes, wanting to fix their circumstances, not noticing some shoes are too small, some tight fitting, others too big, flipping and flopping—you name it—taking on everyone else's hurts and pains that are out of my control.

Self-Forgiveness has transformed my mindset, and now was the time to put respect for myself into further action. Hold myself accountable as I show myself respect. I'm Self-Loving on myself, and it feels so good inside! No more room for negative energy or circumstances that are out of my control, respecting and holding myself accountable with action as I greater Self-Love.

Negative energy is real. You have the ability and power to control your negative energy toward self and others. Words are powerful for me. I find when experiencing negative-energy words—like *sad, mad, anxious, unhappy, stressed,* etc.—I didn't like how these words made me feel within. The air I breathe thickens. Thoughts become cloudy. My body physically breaking down leads me to constantly feeling exhausted and tired. I find a word that's of positive energy and will work for me: disappointed. *Disappointed: defeated in expectation or hope.*

For me, to be disappointed means it is out of my control. It is between the individual—no matter what role they serve within my life or not (stranger, family, friends, acquaintances)—and their ascended master to work out. Being their circumstance is out of my control, I focus back on Self-Love by keeping myself committed to Jesus, choosing to wear my own shoes, careful not to edge God out again, for I am being given another chance to do better and change how I love on myself. Now using my taught and learned strength toward myself in my times of Self-Truth as negative energy is heavy and surfaces upon my body physically. Back, knees, hips—all bodily parts physically hurting. Tired and exhausted most days. I must continue to hold myself accountable for what I can control—self. All while acknowledging that, I, too, am a sinner and not perfect.

> ***Therefore, since we are surrounded by such a great cloud of witnesses, let us throw off everything that hinders and the sin that so easily entangles. And let us run with perseverance the race marked out for us. (Hebrews 12:1 NIV)***

What does it mean to carry each other's burdens, and can you honestly say that this is something you would be willing to do knowingly? You have enough going on in your life. Truth be told, we are taught as children to carry each other's burdens. Most of us have been molded to survive or exist through someone else's perception of how they think your life should look for you, most times, what they failed to accomplish (see *The Four Agreements* by Miguel Ruiz).

When you are willing to allow your Divine power to flow throughout your fleshly bodies, it will amaze you how noncomplex it is to carry each other's burdens once you implement Self-Love. With greater understanding, I've learned that to carry each other's burdens is to show love, compassion and be of encouragement when they are going through difficult and good times. Pray for or with them. Give a sense of hope when they desperately need a breakthrough in their lives. Not by judging them, pulling them down, or making them feel alone during their difficult times because you can't relate. "Hurt people hurt people" is a true saying. We all have been hurt, and therefore, we hurt others knowingly and unknowingly.

We must learn to revert back to the word *love*. Yes, you must be willing to do your part in love. Yes, you must do the work that is required for your change of Self-Love before you can carry others' burdens. Self-Love will allow you to better love others with respect while showing them how to respect who you've chosen to be in this life.

With that said, you may have to experience removing yourself from some people and things within your life to heal. Be hopeful, knowing if it's meant to be in your life, the closed door will reopen if it is a part of your ascended master's plan. Some people and things were removed from my life, yet when the time was right, some of those people and things were given back to me with rewards! The negativity had turned into positivity! Healing on both ends!

It is always a good idea to find one or more like-minded people to journey with you along your Self-Forgiveness, Self-Love, and Self-Care process, those whom you believe you can trust. And if you're thinking there is no one in your life you can trust, think again. Your commitment to Self-Forgiveness and Self-Love should have your mindset in a clearer state. You should have more trust now within yourself. Trusting to know that you have been and are doing the work toward a better you! And it's working for your good! It's manifesting right now, manifesting for you daily! Your ascended master is of great help as you seek trust in others!

NOW FAITH IS BEING SURE

OF WHAT WE HOPE FOR AND CERTAIN

OF WHAT WE DO NOT SEE.

-HEBREWS 11:1

Faith

I have been blessed to have people I can trust in my life. I call them my truth tellers. Their genuine love for me has always come at no cost. Listening when I needed an ear to just listen. Slow to judge me but bold to share their positive energy. Supporting, encouraging, holding my arms up for me in my times of weakness. Helping to build me up when I stumble. They are there in times of different and difficult circumstances. Ready and willing to learn and grow together, agreeing to disagree yet still coming back to the greatest gift—love, love toward one another.

Learning to utilize the greatest gift will take time and will need to be implemented daily. Starting with love toward yourself will be beneficial for your love toward others. Others who genuinely love you will show their action of like-mindedness. And others who are out to destroy, kill, and devour you because of the change within yourself will begin to show through their actions of non-like-mindedness. *"The thief comes only to steal and kill and destroy; I have come that they may have life, and have it to the full" (John 10:10 NIV).*

Do not allow your peace to be disrupted. Hold on to it tightly. The work you implement for Self-Love will teach you how to receive your worth, while showing others your newfound Self-Worth. Yes, you are worthy! *Worth: moral or personal value: to the fullest extent of one's value or ability.* And once you embrace and receive your reward of worth, you will have also received the greatest gift—love. And when circumstances arise, as they will continue to do into your life, refer to the tools that you and your ascended master decided to implement that work best for you. Encourage yourself! Hold yourself accountable, which will help you begin to hold others accountable! You control how to become a better you through your changes and growth with Self-Love, remembering that you are in control of yourself!

BELIEVE

SELF-CARE

Self-Care—the third finger pointing back at you. What people say and do matter to us. Why? Why do we allow others to dictate what our lives should look like and how our lives should be lived? Always feeling as if we just don't fit in, especially if we aren't meeting their requirements. Who are they anyway? Who gave them permission to judge us, and where are they today in their lives? Are they living the life they've molded us into? Why do we care what they have to say about us? These are some questions I asked myself as I began the Self-Care process.

Again, I revert back to my tools that have been working for me, with greater emphasis on my new Self-Foundation—prayer, faith, hope, peace, love, obedience, and trust. At this point in my life, I have witnessed and have been rewarded for my works of Self-Forgiveness and Self-Love with the help of my ascended master, Jesus. Each day begins and ends for me with prayer.

> *Ask and it will be given to you;*
> *seek and you will find; knock*
> *and the door will be opened*

> *to you. For everyone who asks receives; the one who seeks finds; and to the one who knocks, the door will be opened. (Matthew 7:7–8 NIV)*

Ascended Master

Pray, Prayer, Praying

Most of us question, "Why do we need to pray?" "Whom do we pray to?" "What do we pray about?" "How does praying look?" "Does praying really help us?"

Pray, prayer, praying is to make a request in a humble manner, to address God or a god with adoration, confession, supplication, or thanksgiving. Communication is key with your ascended master, as well as listening. Praying to your ascended master will allow you to open your heart and truly share your ups and downs of your life—Self-Truths. Confess your wrongdoings. Release the truths that have caused you pain and hurt. Engage in a loving fellowship with your ascended master who's without judgment.

Jesus, my ascended master, said,

> *And when you pray, do not be like the hypocrites, for they love to pray standing in the synagogues and on the street corners to be seen by others. Truly, I tell you, they have received their reward in full. But when you pray, go into your room, close the door and pray to your Father, who is unseen. Then your Father, who sees what is done in secret, will reward you. And when you pray, do not keep*

on babbling like pagans, for they think they will be heard because of their many words. Do not be like them, for your Father knows what you need before you ask him.

This, then, is how you should pray:

"Our Father in heaven,
hallowed be your name,
your kingdom come,
your will be done,
on earth as it is in heaven.
Give us today our daily bread.
And forgive us our debts, as we also have forgiven our debtors.
And lead us not into temptation, but deliver us from the evil one." (Matthew 6:5–13 NIV)

The prayer instructions from Jesus are where I started on who, what, where, why, and how I would pray in my life. A daily effort of reading His instructions, I then began to meditate for greater understanding as to how prayer would be implemented in growth as I began to grow. Listening, I heard Jesus respond to my prayers, and I started to communicate with Him more throughout each day. Some would say I am talking to myself, yet I know all is well with me in my new season! My mind has been transformed. I'm comfortable with the woman I have become.

How you choose to pray is up to you. Many will give you advice that they themselves more than likely do not practice. I pray as it comes to me. I may be lying in or across my bed praying, on my knees at times, while driving, cooking, bathing, etc. I have chosen to be in constant communication with Jesus. Answers for my questions of who, what, where, why, and how I pray.

At this point in my new season of self, I have memorized the four agreements by Miguel Ruiz, saying them out loud, sometimes several times a day. The four agreements are an impactful tool to help you with getting back to Self-Care daily. Learning to navigate your own positive energy is powerful. Self-Power to redirect any negative energy trying to sneak in and take you away from your positive energy.

> *No weapon forged against you will prevail, and you will refute every tongue that accuses you. This is the heritage of the servants of the Lord, and this is their vindication from me, declares the Lord. (Isaiah 54:16b–17 NIV)*

Show up for yourself and be ready so you don't have to get ready. ***"Accept what is. Let go of what was. And have faith in what will be" (unknown author)***. Negativity is hardwired into us as children. We are taught from a young age to how to protect / stand up for ourselves. Taking the focus off the good within ourselves because we are always faced with what others say is not of good about us, leading us down the road of negative thoughts about ourselves. Learning to Self-Care from within will require you to embrace your weaknesses. Showing weakness and vulnerability will allow you to become stronger from within.

> ***But he said to me, "My grace is sufficient for you, for my power is made perfect in weakness." Therefore I will boast all the more gladly about my weaknesses, so that Christ's power may rest on me. That is why, for Christ's sake I delight in weaknesses, in insults, in hardships, in persecutions, in difficulties. For when I am weak, then I am strong. (2 Corinthians 12:9–10 NIV)***

Exercise is another tool that is working for my good. I had gained over sixty pounds. Every part of my body is in physical pain, unhealthy from my head to my toes, carrying the weight of the world upon me. *Diet* is not a word in my vocabulary today. Like me, I'm sure you've tried every diet out there. Because I'm adamant about doing better for myself, I prayed and asked for direction on what God has planned for me regarding exercise. What He knows will work best for the fearfully and wonderfully made body He created, not created to survive or exist but created to live a good, happy life.

I pray on the concerns throughout my body. My lower back from a shifted vertebrae from large breasts that I had reduced years ago. Ears feeling plugged from throat issues of postnasal drip. Esophagus eroding from acid reflux. Stomach bulging from golf-ball-size hernias that need to be repaired. Daily nausea. Heart arrhythmia—irregular beats within five different areas of my heart. A surgical ablation procedure done that didn't work to help repair my heart. My body breaking down, causing me not to be able to eat. During the Self-Forgiveness process, I forgave myself for neglecting to care for my body. Waiting patiently for direction, I was ready to commit to whatever needed to be done to help heal my body. Some of these concerns were taken care of through surgical procedures, while others healed miraculously!

I came across a few DVDs I had purchased years ago for exercise. Going through them, one stood out—yoga for beginners. *Yoga, a Hindu theistic philosophy teaching the suppression of all activity of body, mind, and will in order that the self may realize its distinction from them and attain liberation. And a system of physical postures, breathing techniques, and sometimes meditation derived from Yoga but often practiced independently, especially in Western cultures to promote physical and emotional well-being.*

I prayed. I listened. I began a twelve-week self-challenge of yoga. Had to be God's plan. I remember purchasing the DVD years ago. And after watching it, I had come to the conclusion that I wouldn't be able to do the majority of the poses. Hadn't even tried to do them. How quickly I allowed negative energy to overpower my positive energy. Yoga is the exercise I practice almost daily. Within several weeks of my challenge, I noticed how clear my mind was becoming. I felt comfort and peace each day as I did the work of Self-Care with yoga as my exercise.

A peaceful place of meditation over my mind and body is what yoga does for me, seeing before my eyes the weight of the world physically falling off my body. Down thirty pounds and feeling fully healed. Body organs restored, functioning at their highest capacity. Some medications no longer needed. Feeling my inner body working for the good of my outer body. Hair strong and growing. A smile across my face that expands from ear to ear. Skin smooth and glowing. Shoulders back and head held high. Receiving my reward of blessing, knowing my Self-Care work has had a huge impact as well. Yes, it's okay to pat yourself on the back! You must take action and do your part to help your ascended master with helping you become a better you. And doing my part and taking action with my Self-Forgiveness, Self-Love, and Self-Care led me to my Divine Life's Purpose!

Divinity

YOUR DIVINE LIFE'S PURPOSE

You were given a purpose before you were created, before anyone had an opinion and judged your life. *Purpose: something set up as an object or end to be attained. Biblical purpose: humans are created with the intent of abundant living.*

> **Shout for joy to the Lord, all the earth. Worship the Lord with gladness; come before him with joyful songs. Know that the Lord is God. It is he who made us, and we are his; we are his people the sheep of his pasture. (Psalm 100:1–3)**

God's desire is for us to be His people and for Him to be our everything. He desires redemption for us all while on earth. We must learn and grow through happy and painful life experiences, with free will to choose between good and evil, whether serving others or self.

Finding your purpose in life will have to start with you. You must want to change your mindset of growth to receive and live your purpose. Practice kindness and gratitude. Be thankful for all things. Be willing to give back. Turn your pains into purpose. Spend time with positive people who uplift you. Be aware of your surroundings. Notice positive messages being sent to you through quotes shared even a license plate, billboards, business names, etc. Create affirmations for yourself. Practice using all your senses—sight, touch, taste, hearing, and smelling. Everything around you of positivity is for your good. Prioritize your Self-Forgiveness, Self-Love, and Self-Care tools. Meditate. Speak aloud to hear yourself claim the desires of your heart. Listen to yourself and others without judgment. Be still and rest when needed. Work on being patient as you wait for answers. Be slow to be anxious, and worry less. Do the work for yourself no matter how long it takes.

As a child around the ages of eleven to thirteen, I was told I had the gift of healing. I questioned if she meant voodoo or witchcraft. Maybe she meant a psychic or medium. Because we are taught to fear everything in life, I chose to fear what I had been told, feared what others would think or say. I Self-Sabotaged and suppressed the very gift that was chosen for me. I suppressed my Divine Life's Purpose, which led me down the road of depression and ultimately was one of many reasons why I attempted suicide in my early twenties (see the author's book *Honesty From Within: Memoirs of Love*).

In the past ten years, I took baby steps with my Self-Forgiveness, Self-Love, and Self-Care, which allowed me to be in a place to receive my Divine Life's Purpose—*working with the Ascended Masters, Angels, and Archangels to help others with positive effects of healing throughout the world.* I've even connected with my ancestors! Today, I see, hear, feel, and speak with them all daily as they help me to help others. For everything bad in the world, there's good in the bad. It depends on you and how you choose to react. And everything they've provided has been for my good! No, I do not have a connection with evil spirits; however, I have been blessed to see when they try to surface. Again, what the world has for bad, God provides good that overpowers with authority and always wins!

Look for Angels and Archangels in your life; they are everywhere! They may be within a pet you have, someone you physically encounter, a whisper in your ear, an encouraging thought that crosses your mind, clear or colorful sparkles in your vision, a hug you second-guess when you're feeling alone. One of many things the Angels and Archangels have shared with me is that they need for us to ask them for help, as they cannot and will not force their help.

Be ready once you ask them to help you! They get excited like a little kid in the candy store! Your life will begin to change for the better! Barriers you couldn't break will begin to crumble right before your eyes! Positive changes will occur. You will no longer feel as if you are trying to survive or exist. You will feel free and truly living your best life! The fourth and final finger pointing back at you.

Enjoy
the
LITTLE THINGS
in
Life!

Conclusion

Someone once said, "Life doesn't give you what you want, but it gives you what you need," and "Without risks, there's no rewards." We all have a part or role to participate in within our lives. Our obedience to our ascended master is crucial. My God works on my behalf as I do the work and will of His obedience. What the world has for bad, God provides good for it, good to outweigh our bad life experiences to help guide us while living on earth as peacefully as possible individually and collectively.

Once you commit to doing the work of Self-Forgiveness, Self-Love, and Self-Care daily, you will live with greater peace, joy, love, comfort, and happiness each day of your life, transforming the renewing of your mindset. Here's my prayer for you: May you grow in Self-Forgiveness, Self-Love, and Self-Care with gratitude and thanksgiving. Accept who you have been created to be with your unique gifts and talents. May you find peace in your good, bad, and ugly circumstances through your Divine Life's journey. In Jesus's name, amen.

Enter through the narrow gate. For wide is the gate and broad is the road that leads to destruction, and many enter through it. But small is the gate and narrow the road that leads to life, and only a few find it. (Matthew 7:13 NIV)

Acknowledgments

I give honor, glory, and praise to my higher power, God, the one who leads and guides me each day to be a blessing to others while being blessed!

I thank the Angels and the Archangels for their guidance with helping me with my Self-Forgiveness, Self-Love, and Self-Care, which led me to my Divine Life's Purpose.

The beauty of being blessed with three beautiful children—DeVontae, Dominique, and DeJarae. Thank you for trusting me as your earthly mother and for loving me through the mistakes I have made as your mom. My parents, Gary and Lorie, for your patience, support, and love.

Jennifer Hudson, for inspiring me with her words of "utilizing your platform" on her September 28, 2022, show. And various guests who have been encouraging and empowering as they stood out on faith and have been blessed while being a blessing to others.

For God so loved the world that
he gave his one and only Son,
that whoever believes in him

shall not perish but have eternal life. For God did not send his Son into the world to condemn the world, but to save the world through him. (John 3:16–17)

About the Author

Since publishing her first book, *Honesty From Within: Memoirs of Love*, in 2013, many people have asked if and when Zelda Bendinger would write another book. In her heart, she felt and knew she would write again. She had mind battles on what she should write about. A few years ago, her daughter suggested that she should consider writing a book of encouragement as she has been and still is an encouragement to so many people.

With prayer and her own self-forgiveness, self-love, and self-care journey, she felt inspired to begin the process of another book. On May 5, 2023, she clearly heard from the Angels and Archangels, "Your Divine Life's Purpose involves working with the Angels and Archangels to help others!" In that moment, she questioned, "Why me?" Then without hesitation, she spoke out loud, "Why not me!" She was visited by an angel who revealed to Zelda that she would help assist with the writing of this book.

Zelda's prayer is to help others see themselves as the Divinely created individuals that they are while living their best life day by day, starting today!